ECHOES OF CHRISTMAS

(His advent and our blessing)

Martin K. Obeng

Amazon

ISBN:9798300023058

Cover design by: Dall-E
Library of Congress Control Number: 2018675309
Printed in the United States of America

This book is dedicated to all my friends and colleagues and all those who subscribe to my poetry blog (cofysbitznpieces.com). This work is also dedicated especially to the loving memory of Edwin H. Simmons Jr, who encouraged me to write poetry in my native language, Twi and always cheered me on.

The true meaning of Christmas is not so much about the celebration of the birth of Jesus as it is about the celebration of the life of Jesus. -Dietrich Bonhoeffer

Christmas is not a time nor a season, but a state of mind. To cherish peace and goodwill, to be plenteous in mercy, is to have the real spirit of Christmas.- John Wesley

CONTENTS

INTRODUCTION

This book is all about the Christmas theme. It is an odd collection of 56 poems. The poetry has been written mainly in an 11-year span. The poems are arranged in chronological order. The poems touch on the Christmas story by way of personalities like Mary and Joseph, the Angel Gabriel, Herod, the shepherds, wisemen etc. They also mention the setting -Bethlehem, Jerusalem etc. The key importance of this season and its celebration is highlighted in the poetry. This is the fact that Jesus had to be born first, before He could grow up into a man, and one day give His life as a sacrifice for the salvation of mankind.

I invite you on this breathtaking tour, pilgrimage etc to relive the great events of Christmas through this collection. I trust you will be greatly blessed in so doing.

PREFACE

After mulling over what to do with all the Christmas poetry I have written over the years, besides those I publish regularly on my poetry blog (cofysbitznpieces.com), I decided to take some positive action. This collection is solely on the theme of Christmas which is celebrated directly and indirectly by mainly Christians and others.

Growing up in a Christian family, Christmas was one of the festivities we engaged in and thoroughly enjoyed. As children we knew we could look forward to new clothes, gifts etc. There were always the special foods cooked at home and the many parties we sometimes attended in friends' homes.

From enjoying the season and participating in church plays on the Advent, singing carols etc, I got to know all about Christmas and the main characters involved so to speak. As an adult I have learnt the real significance of the event and its importance to Christianity - without the birth there could be no death and salvation for us all.

It is my wish and prayer that this collection will be a blessing to all who pick up and read any or all these poems.

CHAPTER ONE

As the bells of the Yuletide chime

To usher in this wonderful time

And God smiles down on his children

For His beautiful Gift to the brethren

(12/10/82)

Oh God, we thank you for this event

Without which our world would be poorer

For our lives have become richer

Because of your Great Gift

(12/10/82

The Wisemen

It was not beneath their dignity

For Wisemen to travel from afar

To come to worship and adorn

No less than the Savior

Of the world

(12/06/84)

The Shepherds

In the stillness of a cold night

Shepherds go to pay their

Due homage to the

New –born Savior

(12/06/84)

The Savior

A Savior in a manger born

The beginning of the

Salvation of a depraved world

A grateful world's thanks

To God

What a Savior

(12/06/84)

CHAPTER TWO

Christmas Ingredients

If you have a prophecy

If you take a star

If you take a town

Called Bethlehem

If you take a willing

Mary and obedient Joseph

If you take an inn keeper

And a manger

If you take some shepherds

With sheep at night

If you take wisemen

With their gold, frankincense

And myrrh

Then you have a

Christmas

(12/23/12)

Merry Christmas

Isaiah

800 seasons

Angel Gabriel

Mary Virgin

Joseph father

Baby Jesus

Bethlehem village

Shepherds watching

Angels speaking

Star shining

Wisemen giving

Merry Christmas

(12/23/12)

Bethlehem

Quiet village

Small village

Great village

Hosted the Messiah

Visited by Wisemen

Your mention is

International

Your mention is

Perpetual

(12/29/12

Who will look in Judah?

Who will look in Judah?

Who will look in Samaria?

Who will look in Jerusalem?

Who will look in Galilee?

For the new-born Savior

They wouldn't find anywhere else

In Bethlehem only

Can He be found

In Bethlehem only

Was it so prophesied

(12/29/12)

Room for us all

There was no room

In the inn itself

Except the lowly manger

For the Savior to be born

Yet through His

Birth and death

He created a room

For us all

To find His pardon

To find His peace

To find His salvation

To find a future Home

(12/29/12)

CHAPTER THREE

Christmas

Even though it often turns
To happy holidays
Because of Hannukah
And others

The season will never
Be lost on us
For carols will still
Be played and sung
In church and
Everywhere else
To remind us all
That
It's still
Merry Christmas
(12/8/13)

The Overlooked

The Big Message

Of a Great Birth

Was sent through

The overlooked in

Society

The shepherds

To get to us all

A Savior has been

Born

(12/24/13)

A Star

A Star unnamed

A light to lead

A beacon to guide

A mystery to be revealed

A Savior born

(12/24/13)

A Light

To them that sit in

Darkness

To them that sorrow

Envelopes

To them that despair

Surrounds

To them that sit in

Uncertainty

To them that are affected by

Conflict

A Light has dawned

A Change has entered

A Christ child has been

Born

Jesus

(12/24/13)

CHAPTER FOUR

Without the angels

Studying geology

Without rocks

Studying math

Without numbers

Studying art

Without colors

Studying chemistry

Without chemicals

Studying music

Without encountering sound

Is like

Christmas without

The angels

Something critical

Would be really missing

(12/4/14)

Where is the baby?

Where is the baby?

Where is the baby?

Jesus

In the midst of

The shoppers

In the midst of

The celebration

In the midst of

The clamor

In the midst of

The glitz

In the midst of

The glamour

In the midst of

All that goes on

In the name of Christmas

Often being called

The holidays

Let's go look

For Him

The Missing One

In it all

To adore

Him always

(12/4/14)

Hear the angels

Hear the angels

Singing

Hear the heavenly

Lilt

Hear the divine

Chorus

Hear the sound of Heaven

Never before heard

On this side of

Eternity

Announcing the

Arrival of the

Heavenly Babe

The King of Kings

Hush

Hush

Hush

(12/16/14)

CHAPTER FIVE

Messages of Christmas

Immanuel

He is with Us

The Manger

God can go low for us.

We must be humble.

The Shepherds

God always leads

and protects Us.

The Angels

God never stops speaking

to Us.

He doesn't leave us

in the dark.

Mary and Joseph

God deals and works

with us even if

we are regular folk.

The Star

God guides and guards Us.

His leading is always certain.

Bethlehem

God uses the lowly

and forgotten.

Quirinius

God uses rulers to fulfil

His ends.

The heart of the king

is directed by Him.

Inn Keeper

God will visit you

and you may not know.

Wisemen

God has room for the

Wise and powerful

God has His messages

At Christmas

(11/26/16

Christmas actors

The prophets

The Governor

The angels

The couple –

Mary and Joseph

The Inn keeper

The shepherds

The wisemen

The beneficiaries-

Us all

Wow

(11/26/16)

Hail Jesus

Hail baby

In the manger

Hail King

In the manger

Hail Messiah

Revealed to us

Hail Savoir

On the cross

Hail Returning Monarch

To take us to Heaven

Hail, hail, hail

(12/18/16)

Beautiful Story

Angel Gabriel
Appears to Mary
A Godly Son to be born
Joseph in a dream assured

The fullness of time
Compelled by a Roman census
Mary and Joseph
To lowly Bethlehem
They proceeded

The Baby Jesus

Being born in a manger

The promise of God

Fulfilled for us all

Salvation and deliverance

Has come

What a Story!

(12/18/16)

CHAPTER SIX

Christmas story

Story of glory

Story of might

Story of wonder

Story of salvation

Story of worship

Story of peace

Story of destiny

Story of love

Story of faithfulness

Story of caring

Story of protection

At Christmas

And always

(11/26/17)

Worship

Worship the baby King

Worship the Coming Redeemer

Worship the Coming Savior

Worship

Worship

Worship

Worship

Worship Jesus

At Christmas

(11/26/17)

The actors

The angels

Who sang in worship

The Romans

Who ordered what led to worship

The Couple

Whose worship was obedience

The shepherds

Who ran to worship

The inn keeper

Whose worship was a manger provided

The wise men

Who journeyed to worship

All played their part in their worship

Worship the Savior

(11/26/17)

Season for comers

Come

To see the Savior

Come

To adore the Savior

Come

To worship the Savior

Come

To exult the Savior

Come

To present yourself to the Savior

Come

To praise the Savior

This Christmas

(11/26/17)

The Season

Season of Beginnings

Season of joy

Season of challenges

Season of a birth

Season of a journey

Season of celebration

Season of remembrance

Season of prophecy fulfillment

Season of Christmas

Jesus is the reason

(12/3/17)

He is the reason

He is the reason

For the season

No matter the season

What happens in the season

Whichever is the season

Jesus is the reason

For all seasons

(12/3/17)

CHAPTER SEVEN

The cries of Christmas

The sheep bleating

The cattle lowing

The virgin crying

The shepherds screaming

The angels singing

The shepherds rejoicing

The wise men worshipping

(12/21/18)

The dream of Christmas

The dream of prophets

The dream of a people

The dream of a nation

The dream of generations

The dream of ancients

The dream of Mankind

The dream comes true

The Christ Child

The Messiah

The Savior

Is born

The dream comes true

What a blessing

(12/19/18

The lights of Christmas

The lights of anticipation

The lights of excitement

The lights of contemplation

The lights of comfort

The lights of reassurance

The lights of joy

The lights of salvation

The lights of Christmas

(12/21/18)

CHAPTER EIGHT

Sign of Christmas

A baby wrapped

Swaddling cloths

Lying in a manger

God's inexplicable gift

Wrapped in humility

Available to all humanity

(12/21/19)

Christmas environment

Baby Messiah

Obedient parents

Mary and Joseph

Humble and surprised

Rejoicing shepherds

Exulting angels

Amazed residents

of Bethlehem

Wonderful news

That had to be proclaimed

(12/21/19)

Christmas names

Jesus

Emmanuel

Wonderful Counsellor

Mighty God

Everlasting Father

Prince of Peace

Messiah

(12/21/19)

Christmas summary

God's glory

In our lives

His peace

In our hearts

Living to please Him

Our goal

(12/21/19)

Wonderful Counsellor

With Wonderful news

To Wonderful shepherds

By Wonderful angels

About a Wonderful plan

Through Wonderful parents

Providing a Wonderful Savior

Giving us a Wonderful Christmas

Counsellor extraordinary

Mighty God

Mighty of God of Creation

Mighty God of Providence

Mighty God of Salvation

Mighty God of Eternity

Mighty God of Everything

Mighty God of Christmas

Everlasting Father

Everlasting guidance

Everlasting support

Everlasting provision

Everlasting good news

Everlasting Savior

Everlasting Christmas

Prince of Peace

Peace at home

Peace at work

Peace delivered

Peace enabled

Peace always

Peace Divine

Peace at Christmas

(12/23/19)

CHAPTER NINE

The Star

Star of the East

Star of revelation

Star of guidance

Star of destiny

Star of hope

May your brightness

May your great light

Illuminate

Our paths

our lives

our endeavors

This time

And always

(12/18/20)

The Gift @Christmas

God's perfect Gift

God's inexpressible Gift

God's wonderful Gift

Bestowed upon us

Blessed on us

By our merciful God

By our generous God

At this great time

God is good

(12/18/20)

The Baby -Jesus

Innocence

Power

Wonder

Splendor

Majesty

Hope

Salvation

Ushered upon

Us

Christmas

Cherished

(12/18/20

The Son

Son of man

Son of God

Son of destiny

Son of blessing

Son of deliverance

Enter

Into our lives

Our circumstances

Our world

Our lives

This Christmas

And always

(12/18/20)

Christmas haiku

Christmases past and present

Much to contemplate and

Wonder

(12/18/20)

Savior of the world entering

As infant into a troubled universe

To save man

(12/18/20)

Cattle low, sheep bleat, clear skies, still

Night Bethlehem ushers in

The King of kings

(12/18/20)

A Star among stars, wisemen among the wise

An odyssey provoked culminating in

A wonderful journey

(12/18/20)

Bright night skies, heavenly host,

Angelic column herald the

Entry of the baby King

(12/18/20)

A different way

The wisemen

Took a different way

To depart

When they heard

His voice

May we also take

a different way

when needed

to return

to depart

when we hear

His voice

(12/20/20)

CHAPTER TEN

Away...

Away from Santa Claus

Away from the reindeers

Away from the snow

Away from the jingle bells

Away from the Christmas trees

Lies the baby

Lies the Mighty God

Lies the Jesus Christ

A Savior is born

The most wonderful

Time of the year

Merry Christmas

(12/23/21)

It's all about the Son

A virgin gives birth

To a Son

The Son is called Jesus

The Son of the Highest

The Son is the King

The Son is the Mighty God

The Son is the Prince of peace

The Son is the Wonderful Counsellor

The Son is the Light

The Son is the Savior

A Son is born

Thank God

for Christmas

(12/23/21)

The Government

The Government upon His shoulder

The Government of the hearts of men

The Government that usher in peace

The Government that saves the people

The Government of Jesus

Christmas in perspective

(12/23/21)

CHAPTER ELEVEN

Room @ Christmas

There was no room

At the inn

There was no room

For Jesus

To be born

May we always

Find room

In our hearts

In our lives

In our activities

In our decisions

In our everything

For Jesus

(12/22/22)

Chains break @ Christmas

The chains

Of worry

The chains

Of desperation

The chains

Of affluence

The chains

Of poverty

The chains

Of ill health

The chains

Of this life

Jesus breaks

Every chain

At Christmas

(12/22/22)

Happiness @Christmas

A world in centuries anticipation

A Savior is born

A world is comforted

A world is relieved

Happiness has arrived

Happiness has been born

Happiness has brought hope

Happiness has brought light

Happiness has brought justice

Happiness has brought peace

Happiness has brought reconciliation

Happiness is Jesus

Happiness came with Christmas

(12/22/22)

Peace @ Christmas

Peace perfect peace

The Prince of peace

The King of peace

The Lord of peace

Jesus is peace

Jesus brings peace

At Christmas

(12/22/22)

Joy @ Christmas

The joy of the angels

The joy of the shepherds

The joy of the people

The joy of the oppressed

The joy of the weak

The joy of the mighty

The joy of the wealthy

The joy of the poor

The joy of humanity

Jesus brings joy

At Christmas

(12/22/22)

Buronya ato y3n

Buronya ato y3n

Won awo Oba barima no

Buronya ato y3n

Won awo Agyenkwa no

Buronya ato y3n

Won awo asomdwoe

Buronya ato y3n

Won awo anigye

Buronya ato y3n

Won awo nkwagye

Buronya ato y3n

Won awo anidaso

Buronya

Buronya

Buronya

Onyakopon y3 da w'ase

Mma buronya

(12/22/22)

Christmas is upon us

Christmas is upon us

The Son has been born

Christmas is upon us

The Savior has been born

Christmas is upon us

Peace has been born

Christmas is upon us

Joy has been born

Christmas is upon us

Salvation has been born

Christmas is upon us

Hope has been born

Christmas

Christmas

Christmas

God we thank you

For Christmas

(12/22/22)

Bethlehem

Wo Bethlehem

Amansan da w'ase

Wiase da w'ase

Amaman da w'ase

Wo nna wo gye Agyenkwa taataa

Wo nna wo mma no babi tenae

Wo nna wo hwɛ no so

Wo nna wo tie Onyankopon asƐm

Ɛmma wo yƐ nhyira mma wiase nyinaa

Memma wo afihyia pa

Buronya

Bethlehem

Amansan da w'ase

(12/22/22)

Bethlehem

You, Bethlehem

All and sundry thank you

The whole world thanks you

You protected the Savior

You gave Him a place to stay

You looked after Him

You listened to God's command

So you became a blessing for all

Season's greetings to you

Merry Christmas

Bethlehem

(12/22/22)

CHAPTER TWELVE

Christmas is nigh

When the southern sun begins

To shine down on us

When the nights creep up

So early on us

When the cold, cold winds

Blow upon us

When the bright colorful lights

Begin to shine around us

When the holiday music begins

To waft on us

When the Salvation Army red kettles appear

And the bells rings on us

Christmas is nigh

Christmas is nigh

(11/29/23)

Peace

Peace in our hearts

Peace in our lives

Peace in our homes

Peace in our society

Peace

Peace

Peace

Christmas brings peace

Jesus brings peace

To us all

At Christmas

(12/12/23)

Adore

Adore the divine baby

Adore the coming King of kings

Adore the revealed Lord of lords

Adore the coming Messiah

Adore the coming Savior

Adore

Adore

Adore

Adore Jesus every Christmas

Adore Jesus every day

(12/12/23)

Monnsom

Worship

Monnsom Agyenkwa a won awo no

Worship the newborn Savior

Monnsom Onyame ba abofra a won awo no

Worship the Son of God who has been born

Monnsom Ahene mu ahene a won a awo no

Worship the King of kings who has been born

Monnsom Awura mu awura a won awo no

Worship the Lord of lords who has been born

Monnsom o

Worship

Monnsom o

Worship

Monnsom o

Worship

Monnsom buronya wura

Worship the Lord of Christmas

Buronya bere yi

This Christmas time

(12/12/23)

Let's worship Him

The shepherds went to Bethlehem to worship Him

The angels went up and down worshipping Him

The wisemen laid down their gifts to worship Him

Worship the King

Worship the Messiah

Worship the Savior

Worship Jesus

At Christmas

And always

(12/12/23)

ACKNOWLEDGEMENT

I gratefully acknowledge the support that I have obtained from friends, my Christian family, and others in the work that I have produced and the blessings that have been bestowed on them by the use of my talents. My close family who has always been by my side cannot be left out of my conveyance of sentiments of gratitude.

ABOUT THE AUTHOR

Martin K. Obeng

Martin is a budding author. He originally comes from Ghana in West Africa but now resides with his family in Alexandria, Virginia. This is his third book on poetry. The first being 'The Messages of Christmas' published by Amazon. The second is 'Whispers of Calvary-His Pain, Our victory' also published by Amazon. He also hosts three blogs on his poetry and other writings: cofysthots.blogspot.com; cofysinvocations.wordpress.com; cofysbitznpieces.com. He speaks French, Spanish and a few Ghanaian languages. He is an educator and is married to the love of his life Fanny, and they have a young son, Adomba.

BOOKS BY THIS AUTHOR

The Messages Of Christmas (Published By Amazon) Nov 2023 -Paperback Edition

Messages of Christmas is a delightful and inspiring book for children of all ages. It invites you to experience the Christmas story through the eyes of those who were there, and to celebrate the birth of Jesus Christ, the greatest gift of all.

The Messages Of Christmas (Published By Amazon) Nov 2023 -Kindle Edition

Messages of Christmas is a delightful and inspiring book for children of all ages. It invites you to experience the Christmas story through the eyes of those who were there, and to celebrate the birth of Jesus Christ, the greatest gift of all.

Whispers Of Calvary -His Pain,Our Victory

This book is suitable for people of all ages especially

from early teens to older folk. It spotlights poetry written during a ten -year period. The collection focuses on the important period of Easter which is central to Christianity but can be enjoyed anytime in the year. The poetry is in simple language and broken into chapters to help the reader find their area of interest.

Made in the USA
Columbia, SC
28 December 2025